Custer's Last Stand

Custer's Last Stand

Dennis Brindell Fradin

Marshall Cavendish
Benchmark
New York

Acknowledgment

John A. Doerner, Chief Historian, Little Bighorn Battlefield National Monument

Marshall Cavendish Benchmark
99 White Plains Road
Tarrytown, NY 10591
www.marshallcavendish.us

Text and map copyright © 2007 by Marshall Cavendish Corporation
Map by XNR Productions

Library of Congress Cataloging-in-Publication Data

Fradin, Dennis B.
Custer's last stand / by Dennis Brindell Fradin.
p. cm. — (Turning points of United States history)
Includes bibliographical references and index.
ISBN-13: 978-0-7614-2124-5
ISBN-10: 0-7614-2124-6
1. Little Bighorn, Battle of the, Mont., 1876—Juvenile literature.
2. Custer, George Armstrong, 1839–1876—Juvenile literature. I. Title. II. Series.
E83.876.F63 2006
973.8'2—dc22
2005016020

Photo Research by Connie Gardner

Cover Photo: Kurz & Allison/CORBIS
Title Page: Kurz & Allison/CORBIS
The photographs in this book are used by permission and through the courtesy of: *Corbis:* 18, 22, 34; Geoffrey Clements, 14; W. H. Illingworth, 16;
Bettmann, 6, 24; Tom Bean, 38; Kurz & Allison, 42–43; *The Granger Collection:* 8, 10, 26, 28, 30, 36; *Art Resouce:* Giraudon, 9; *New York Public Library:* Art
Resource, 12; *Getty Images:* MPI Stringer/Hulton Archive, 13, 32; Camillius S. Fly/Hulton Archive, 20; *Brown Brothers:* 25.

Editorial Director: Michelle Bisson
Art Director: Anahid Hamparian
Printed in China
1 3 5 6 4 2

Contents

This Currier and Ives lithograph shows the printing press, telegraph, railroad, and steam engine—proofs of "the progress of the century" since the United States had declared its independence from England.

CHAPTER ONE

The United States Turns One Hundred

The year 1876 was a momentous one in the United States. On July 4, the nation was to celebrate its **centennial**, or one-hundredth birthday. The country's Declaration of **Independence** had been issued exactly a **century** earlier, on July 4, 1776.

The founding fathers would have been amazed to see how the United States had changed in its first century. At first, the country had included just thirteen states and 2.5 million people. By early 1876 there were 45 million people and thirty-seven states, with Colorado about to become the thirty-eighth state later that year.

The building of railroads and steamboats had revolutionized travel by 1876. The development of the **telegraph**, the first device that sent messages by electricity, had transformed communication. Other inventions, from the photograph to the sewing machine, had changed life in the United States.

The nation's Centennial Exposition was hosted in the Art Gallery Building in Philadelphia.

A facsimile of Alexander Graham Bell's original telephone, housed in a Parisian museum.

FAC-SIMILÉ DU TÉLÉPHONE ORIGINAL D'ALEXANDRE GRAHAM BELL
CONSTRUIT PAR LA "WESTERN ELECTRIC C°."
OFFERT PAR LA SOCIÉTÉ ANONYME "LE MATÉRIEL TÉLÉPHONIQUE"

To celebrate the country's hundredth birthday, Philadelphia, Pennsylvania, hosted the Centennial Exposition, which opened in May 1876. A highlight of this World's Fair occurred on June 25 when Alexander Graham Bell demonstrated his new invention: the telephone.

The removal of the Cherokee Indians to reservations in the West in 1838 was known as the "Trail of Tears" because they had to leave their homelands.

CHAPTER TWO

What Happened to the Indians

One group of Americans was in no mood to celebrate the centennial. Starting in colonial times, and continuing throughout the nation's first century, Native Americans had been cheated out of their homelands. Often, white settlers talked them into selling their lands at low prices. When the Indians wouldn't sell, the settlers raised armies and took what they wanted.

Whole tribes were pushed off their lands and sometimes wiped out. The Indians who survived fights with the soldiers were gradually forced to live on **reservations**. Located mainly in the nation's western half, these were

In the 1870s, most of the remaining Native Americans had to leave their land and settle on reservations.

U.S. government agents gave the Assiniboines tribe a year's worth of goods in return for their withdrawal to a reservation. This agreement was part of the Fort Laramie Treaty of 1851.

lands set aside for the Indians by the government. Reservation Indians often suffered from hunger, disease, and other hardships. The result was that, as the white population soared, that of the Indians plunged.

Around the year 1500, a few million Indians lived in what is now the United States. The number had dwindled to about 250,000 in 1865. The bulk of the Native Americans had gone to live on reservations by then.

The Buffalo Hunter, by Seth Eastman, depicts the rare sight of a Native American still roaming his lands freely in the mid–1800s.

CHAPTER THREE

"One Does Not Sell the Earth"

In one part of the country, about 100,000 Indians still roamed freely in 1865. This region, the Great Plains, included parts of Montana, North and South Dakota, Wyoming, Nebraska, Colorado, Kansas, New Mexico, Oklahoma, and Texas. The Sioux, Cheyenne, Arapaho, Comanche, Arikara, and Crow were among the Great Plains tribes. Superb horseback riders, the Plains Indians traveled about hunting **buffalo**, also called bison. They ate buffalo meat and made clothes and tepees from buffalo skins.

In 1874, an Army **expedition** led by Lieutenant Colonel George Armstrong Custer found gold in South Dakota's Black Hills, a sacred place to the Sioux Indians. Just a few years earlier, in 1868, the Sioux had been promised that

the Black Hills would be theirs forever, but the discovery of gold changed everything. In 1875, as thousands of miners poured into the region, the U.S. government tried to convince the Sioux to sell the Black Hills. They refused.

"One does not sell the earth upon which the people walk," said Crazy Horse, a Sioux chief.

In 1874, Lieutenant Colonel George Armstrong Custer led an Army expedition to South Dakota's Black Hills and found gold.

Sitting Bull

Sitting Bull was born around 1831 somewhere in South Dakota. One of his greatest achievements was uniting several Great Plains tribes to fight the white people. He did not actually fight in the Battle of the Little Bighorn. As a **spiritual** leader, he prayed for victory during the battle and directed the women and children in the Indians' camp to places of safety.

"I do not want to sell any land to the government," said Sitting Bull, a Sioux leader. Picking up a bit of dirt off the ground, Sitting Bull added, "not even as much as this!"

The U.S. government decided to seize the Black Hills. In December 1875 the government ordered the Sioux and Cheyenne who lived there to move to reservation lands. Those who refused would be considered "**hostiles**" and would be subject to attack by U.S. troops.

Defying the order, thousands of Sioux and Cheyenne gathered in Montana to hunt buffalo and antelope and protect themselves from U.S. soldiers. Leaders of this huge gathering included Sitting Bull, Crazy Horse, Gall of the Sioux, and Two Moons of the Cheyenne. By late spring of 1876, nearly seven thousand Indians were camped in southeastern Montana.

An expedition to fight the "hostile" Indians who did not want to give up their land was organized by General Alfred H. Terry.

Meanwhile, the U.S. Army organized an expedition to fight the "hostile" Indians. Commanded by General Alfred H. Terry, the expedition was divided into several columns that were to attack the Indians from different directions. The Seventh **Cavalry**, a regiment of horse soldiers, was one of the units. The Seventh was led by Lieutenant Colonel George Armstrong

Custer, who had commanded the Black Hills expedition two years earlier.

Custer led his men out of Fort Abraham Lincoln in North Dakota in May 1876. After an **approximately** four-hundred-mile (600-kilometer) trip that took more than a month, they approached the huge Indian encampment in southeastern Montana. The expedition's other units also approached the "hostile" Indians at about that time.

In mid-June of 1876, Cheyenne hunters spotted a column of "Bluecoats," as they called the soldiers. Led by General George Crook, this column of the Army expedition had entered Montana from Wyoming to the south. A thousand Sioux and Cheyenne warriors mounted their horses and rode out to fight Crook and his men.

Crazy Horse and Two Moons commanded the Indian warriors on this

The Love of War

George Armstrong Custer was born in New Rumley, Ohio, on December 5, 1839. He taught school for a while before attending the United States Military Academy at West Point, New York, where he graduated last in his class in 1861. Twelve horses were shot out from under him during the Civil War, giving him a reputation as a daring cavalry officer. He then became the leader of the Seventh Cavalry, a regiment of Indian fighters formed in 1866. Custer once wrote to a cousin about his love of war: "I would be willing, yes glad, to see a battle every day during my life."

General George Crook (third from right) tries unsuccessfully to persuade the American Indian chief, Geronimo, to move to a reservation.

day—June 17, 1876. The Indians kept on the move constantly, making repeated charges against the Bluecoats. During the battle, a horse was shot out from under Chief-Comes-in-Sight, a Cheyenne warrior. Within moments his sister, **Buffalo**-Calf-Road-Woman, galloped up and rescued him on her horse.

Ten soldiers were killed and twenty-one were wounded in this fight, which the whites called the Battle of the Rosebud because it was fought along Montana's Rosebud Creek. The victorious Indians called it the Battle Where the Girl Saved Her Brother.

Eight days later, the Indians and the soldiers would fight a much larger and more famous battle.

Crazy Horse

Crazy Horse was born in a Sioux village, reportedly in South Dakota around 1840. Those who met him claimed that there was something mystical about the famous Sioux chief. Only one known photograph was taken of Crazy Horse, who believed— as was common among American Indians—that the white man's camera would snatch away his spirit. Crazy Horse married a Cheyenne woman, which gave him an alliance with that tribe.

Sioux leader Sitting Bull was the spiritual leader of the Native Americans' fight against General Custer.

CHAPTER FOUR

"I Am Going to Attack"

Following the fight along the Rosebud, the Indians moved their encampment a short way to the valley of Montana's Little Bighorn River. More Indians joined them. Soon there were 7,000 Native American men, women, and children, including about 2,500 warriors, camped along the Little Bighorn.

On Saturday, June 24, 1876, Indian lookouts told their leaders that more than 600 Bluecoats were headed their way. Sitting Bull was the main Indian leader at the Little Bighorn. A noted Sioux warrior from age fourteen, by 1876 Sitting Bull was a political and religious leader who communicated with the spirit world through dreams and prayers. Before the Bluecoats' approach, Sitting Bull had a vision that the Great Spirit was sending the soldiers into the Indians' camp to be slaughtered.

As at Rosebud Creek, Chief Crazy Horse of the Sioux was one of the leaders of the warriors along the Little Bighorn. Crazy Horse, whose dreams of wild horses had inspired his name, had vowed to fight the Bluecoats to the death, and had engaged in several battles with them. Yet among his own people, Crazy Horse was known for his kindness and generosity. It was said that, except for his weapons and a few other items, he had given all his belongings to the needy.

Chief Crazy Horse was one of the leaders of the Native Americans who fought against Custer at the Battle of the Little Bighorn.

George Armstrong Custer, commander of the more than six hundred approaching Seventh Cavalry troops, guides, interpreters, and other aides, was a colorful and **controversial** officer. The Sioux called Lieutenant Colonel Custer "Long Yellow Hair" because he sometimes wore his hair in long curls. He was also called the "Boy General" because he had temporarily achieved that rank at age twenty-three during the Civil War. While many Seventh Cavalry members admired his bravery, others thought that Custer was overly interested in personal glory. It was said that he believed a victory over the Indians would help elect him president of the United States.

In his pocket Custer carried General Alfred Terry's instructions. Terry advised him to wait for the rest of the expedition before attacking the Indians, but added that Custer was free to use his own judgment. On the morning of June 25—the Sunday the telephone was demonstrated approximately two thousand miles (3,218 km) to the east—Custer's scouts brought him some news. The largest encampment of Indians they had ever seen stood along the Little Bighorn River.

General George Armstrong Custer was the commander of the more than six hundred troops that attacked at the Little Bighorn.

Captain Frederick W. Benteen commanded part of the forces at Little Bighorn.

Deciding to attack without waiting for assistance, Custer divided his forces into four groups. He ordered about 135 men to guard the pack mules that carried the Seventh Cavalry's ammunition and supplies. He ordered Captain Frederick W. Benteen and about 125 men to cut off the Indians' escape route to the south. And he ordered Major Marcus A. Reno and about 140 men to attack one portion of the Indian encampment. That left Custer with little more than 200 men to make the major attack.

Major Marcus Reno and his troops tried to attack a large Indian force near Little Bighorn, but about one-third of his forces were killed by the American Indians.

CHAPTER FIVE

The Battle of the Little Bighorn

At midday on June 25, the Indians saw a cloud of dust and the flash of equipment in the distance as the Seventh Cavalry charged their camp. Indian warriors climbed onto their ponies and rode out to fight the Bluecoats.

The battle began around 3 p.m. when Major Marcus Reno and his men encountered a large Indian force near the Little Bighorn. As the warriors barraged them with bullets and arrows, Reno ordered his outnumbered troops to withdraw through the woods. The Indians pursued them. By the time Reno and his men found refuge on a hill, about forty soldiers had been killed or wounded.

Suddenly, as the word spread that Lieutenant Colonel George Custer and his troops were nearby, the Indians turned their attention away from Reno's forces. About a thousand Indian warriors converged on Custer and his men. Crazy Horse and Two Moons led their warriors from one side. Gall and his braves charged the Bluecoats from another. Having suffered so much at the hands of the whites over the years, the Indians felt that they were making a last desperate fight for their liberty. A Sioux leader named Low Dog urged on his warriors by saying: "This is a good day to die. Follow me."

It was mostly the Bluecoats who died that day. The warriors headed toward Custer and his men "like a hurricane, like bees swarming out of a

This pictograph shows Crazy Horse and Sitting Bull mounted on their horses at the Battle of the Little Bighorn.

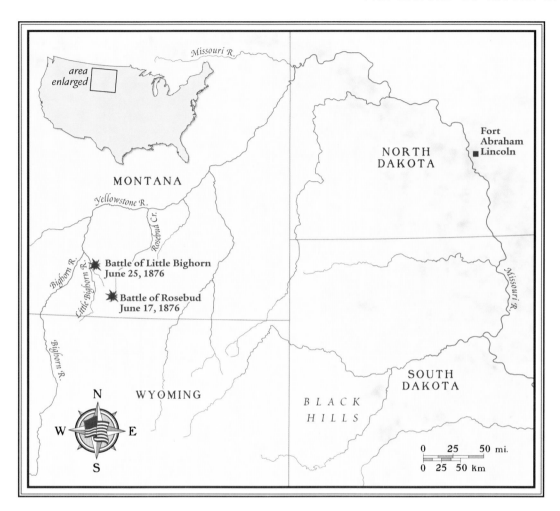

The Battles of Little Bighorn and Rosebud

hive," an Indian leader named Kill Eagle later reported. They attacked the Bluecoats with arrows, bullets, hatchets, and clubs. By the time the sun set, George Armstrong Custer and all the troops with him—some 210 men in all—had been killed. This part of the Battle of the Little Bighorn is known as "Custer's Last Stand."

Native Americans are shown leaving the site of the battle after defeating General Custer and the Seventh U.S. Cavalry. Two of the horses are carrying luggage.

The sole **survivor** of Custer's Last Stand was Comanche, a horse later found on the battlefield with seven wounds. (Comanche lived another fifteen years and became a symbol of pride to the Seventh Cavalry. In 1878 it was ordered that he never be ridden again.)

Meanwhile, Captain Frederick Benteen and his men had joined Major Reno and his surviving troops on the hill. From there, they could hear the sounds of the battle between Custer and the Indians. However, they did not come to Custer's aid.

After destroying Custer's command, the Indians returned to fight Benteen's and Reno's forces, who survived the night by digging pits in the ground in which to hide. The Indians attacked Benteen and Reno's remaining troops at dawn of June 26. The Native Americans were low on ammunition, though, and their scouts reported that more soldiers were on the way. The Indians withdrew later that day. General Terry's troops arrived the next day—June 27—and rescued the survivors of the battle.

In all, about 265 members of the U.S. forces had been killed and 60 had been wounded at the Battle of the Little Bighorn. It was one of the U.S. Army's most famous defeats in its wars against the Indians, and one of the Native Americans' greatest victories against the U.S. Army.

The Fate of the Family

Several of George Armstrong Custer's relatives were killed with him at his "last stand." Among the dead were Custer's brothers, Lieutenant Tom Custer and Boston Custer, who was serving as a guide; Custer's brother-in-law, Lieutenant James Calhoun; and Custer's eighteen-year-old nephew, Henry Armstrong Reed, who was listed as a beef herder but had mostly come along for the excitement.

The bones of the dead are buried on the scene of the Battle of the Little Bighorn.

CHAPTER SIX

Aftermath

News of the battle spread by telegraph around the country. At a time when Americans had expected to celebrate the nation's centennial, they asked each other how the Seventh Cavalry could have suffered such a huge defeat. Nearly everyone had a **theory**.

Some Americans blamed the defeat on Custer's quest for glory. Others accused Major Marcus Reno and Captain Frederick Benteen of not doing enough to rescue Custer and his men, or criticized President Ulysses S. Grant for being "soft" on the Indians. Rather than saying that the soldiers had *lost* the battle, some claimed it was more accurate to admit the Indians had *won* it due to their larger numbers and superior leadership. To this day, people disagree about the reasons for the outcome of the battle.

Sitting Bull sits with his family after he surrendered and moved to a South Dakota reservation. The white woman is Catherine Weldon of Boston, who took an interest in the chief's plight.

In the long run, their triumph at the Little Bighorn proved to be a "last stand" for the Plains Indians, too. The U.S. Army renewed its massive campaign against them, often killing them without cause in the late 1800s. A famous massacre occurred in 1890 at Wounded Knee Creek in South Dakota, where soldiers killed nearly three hundred Sioux.

The Army also targeted Indian leaders. In 1877 Crazy Horse surrendered at a fort in Nebraska. When he realized that he was about to be locked in jail, Crazy Horse struggled to break free. He was killed by a soldier. In 1881 Sitting Bull surrendered. He was imprisoned for two years, then allowed to live on a reservation in South Dakota. In 1890 Sitting Bull was accused of planning another rebellion and was shot to death.

Sitting Bull's death and the Wounded Knee Massacre marked the end of major fighting between the Great Plains Indians and the U.S. Army. By 1890, 190,000 of the nation's 250,000 remaining Indians had been forced onto reservations.

Only 60,000 Native Americans resided on farms and ranches and in towns scattered across the country.

The Buffalo

The Plains Indians' way of life and independence were largely destroyed by white hunters who killed millions of buffalo in the 1800s. By the 1870s white hunters were slaughtering a million buffalo per year. The destruction of these animals—which the Indians had depended on for food, clothing, tepees, and fuel—added to the Native Americans' anger toward the whites.

A memorial to Crazy Horse was carved into the Black Hills in the mid–1990s.

CHAPTER SEVEN

Legend vs. History

Over time, the Battle of the Little Bighorn became known as Custer's Last Stand. Many stories, paintings, and movies were created about the battle.

At first Custer was portrayed as the hero and the Indians as the villains of the battle. Recently, historians have pointed out that the battle was part of the Indians' brave but **futile** struggle to protect their homelands.

The site of the battle was made into a national monument in 1946. Each year, more than 400,000 people visit Little Bighorn Battlefield National Monument in southeastern Montana. They come to see the place where, 130 years ago, George Armstrong Custer and the Plains Indians made their last stand.

Glossary

approximately—About.

buffalo, or bison—Animals weighing up to 3,000 pounds that once roamed North America in large herds.

cavalry—Soldiers who rode to battle on horses.

centennial—A one-hundredth anniversary or birthday.

century—A period of one hundred years.

controversial—Stirring up differences of opinion.

expedition—A group of people who travel together.

futile—Ineffective or producing no useful result.

hostile—Angry, hateful, and bearing ill will; Indians who refused to live on reservations were considered "hostiles."

independence—Freedom, or self-government.

reservations—Areas set aside for Indians by the government.

spiritual—To do with the soul, and religious beliefs.

survivors—Individuals who have remained alive through difficulties.

telegraph—An early device for sending messages by electricity.

theory—Idea or belief.

Timeline

1621—Pilgrims hold famous thanksgiving celebration with the Indians, who have helped them survive

1637—In one of the first wars between colonists and Indians, colonial forces slaughter about 700 Pequots in Connecticut

1830—Congress passes Indian Removal Act, allowing the government to force eastern tribes onto lands west of the Mississippi River

1831—Around this year Sitting Bull is born somewhere in South Dakota

1839—George Armstrong Custer is born in New Rumley, Ohio, on December 5

1840—Crazy Horse is born in about this year, reportedly in South Dakota

1866—Seventh Cavalry, a regiment of Indian fighters, is organized

1868—Sioux Indians are promised that South Dakota's Black Hills will be theirs forever

1874—Army expedition led by Lieutenant Colonel George Armstrong Custer discovers gold in South Dakota's Black Hills

1621   *1839*   *1874*

1875—In December, the U.S. government orders Sioux and Cheyenne Indians onto reservations by January 31, 1876

1876—Spring: Thousands of Sioux and Cheyenne Indians, defying the government's order, camp in southeastern Montana

June 17: Indians under Crazy Horse and Two Moons defeat U.S. forces at the Battle of the Rosebud

June 25-26: Indians organized by Sitting Bull and fighting under Crazy Horse and others win Battle of the Little Bighorn in Montana; Custer's Last Stand on June 25 is the most famous part of the battle

1877—Crazy Horse is murdered by a soldier in Nebraska

1890—The murder of Sitting Bull and the Wounded Knee Massacre, both in South Dakota, deal a crushing blow to the Plains Indians

1976—Hundredth anniversary of Custer's Last Stand

1875　　　　*1877*　　*1976*

Further Information

BOOKS

Cunningham, Chet. *Chief Crazy Horse*. Minneapolis, MN: Lerner, 2000.

Kent, Zachary. *George Armstrong Custer: Civil War General and Western Legend*. Berkeley Heights, NJ: Enslow Publishers, 2000.

Streissguth, Thomas, ed. *Custer's Last Stand*. San Diego: Greenhaven Press, 2003.

WEB SITES

Battle of the Little Bighorn
http://www.eyewitnesstohistory.com/custer.htm

Biography of George Armstrong Custer
http://ohiobio.org/custer.htm

Little Bighorn Battlefield National Monument
http://www.nps.gov/libi/index.htm

PBS biography of Crazy Horse
http://www.pbs.org/weta/thewest/people/a_c/crazyhorse.htm

PBS biography of George Armstrong Custer
http://www.pbs.org/weta/thewest/people/a_c/custer.htm

PBS biography of Sitting Bull
http://www.pbs.org/weta/thewest/people/s_z/sittingbull.htm

Bibliography

Brown, Dee. *Bury My Heart at Wounded Knee: An Indian History of the American West.* New York: Holt, Rinehart & Winston, 1970.

Donovan, Jim. *Custer and the Little Bighorn.* Stillwater, MN: Voyageur Press, 2001.

Sajna, Mike. *Crazy Horse: The Life Behind the Legend.* New York: Wiley, 2000.

Utley, Robert M. *The Lance and the Shield: The Life and Times of Sitting Bull.* New York: Holt, 1993.

Wert, Jeffry D. *Custer: The Controversial Life of George Armstrong Custer.* New York: Simon & Schuster, 1996.

Index

Page numbers in **boldface** are illustrations.

About the Author

Dennis Fradin is the author of 150 books, some of them written with his wife, Judith Bloom Fradin. Their recent book for Clarion, *The Power of One: Daisy Bates and the Little Rock Nine*, was named a Golden Kite Honor Book. Another of Dennis's recent books is *Let It Begin Here! Lexington & Concord: First Battles of the American Revolution*, published by Walker. The Fradins are currently writing a biography of social worker and anti-war activist Jane Addams for Clarion and a nonfiction book about a slave escape for National Geographic Children's Books. Turning Points in U.S. History is Dennis Fradin's first series for Marshall Cavendish Benchmark. The Fradins have three grown children and three young grandchildren.